FOREWORD OPS

JUST ASK

DEVOTIONS FOR THE COACH'S WIFE

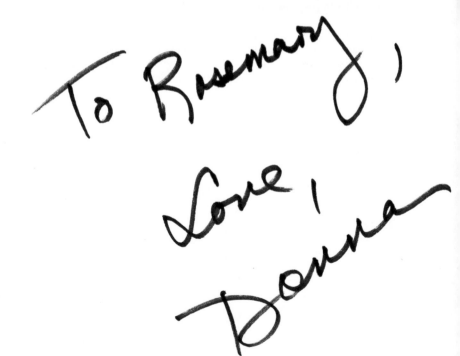

To Rosemary,

Love,
Donna

Just Ask: Devotions for The Coach's Wife

ISBN 978-1-938254-60-4

Cross Training Publishing
www.crosstrainingpublishing.com
(308) 293-3891

Top - Lily

Middle - Sophie Sutphin, Lily

Bottom - Curtis Lofton, Lily

Top - Sophie Sutphin, Lily

Middle - Jake Weldy,
Jennifer Anderson, Marc Ellenburg,
Trey Ellenburg

Bottom - Lily

Table of Contents

Dedication

This book is dedicated to my favorite three coaches' wives! First and foremost, my mom, Sherri Riffe. You are the greatest coach's wife in the whole world! You showed me how to serve your family unselfishly while loving your husband unconditionally...just like Jesus. I want to be just like you when I grow up! Thank you for being the best mom, Christ-like example, and friend a girl could ask for. Love you and "as long as I'm living my momma you'll be."

Second, Kathy Elerick. I watched you so many times as a teacher, mom, and coach's wife wanting your positive attitude, encouraging spirit, and loving heart. The love you and Coach Elerick have for your players, students, and family is inspiring to so many including me! Love you Mrs E!

Third, Jeri Cocannouer. Although you are no longer with us on this earth, your legacy as a coach's wife is eternal. You taught me what it means to love your family, love your husband's players and the whole football staff with such passion and commitment. I will forever take the lessons I learned from you as a coach's wife and mom wherever I go. You will never be forgotten. Love you Jeri C!

Acknowledgements

To Franci MacDonald, Michelle Hooper, Jennifer Sharpe, and Jill Schenk: Thank you for your grace in reading this book and your truth in making changes to it. So thankful for your friendship and examples of inspiration you have been in my life.

To Gordon, Cross Training Publishing, Jeff Martin: Thank you so much for believing in this project! So thankful for you as my teammates!

To my FCA Family: Thank you for being supportive, encouraging, and overall great teammates on the front lines of ministry.

To Donna Noonan, Jami Smith, Shannon Rowe, Laura Clay: You all are the greatest friends, mentors, accountability partners, ministry partners a girl could ask for! I love you dearly!

Thank you to all the women who shared their stories for this book. I am inspired and encouraged by your courage, love, hearts you have for your families and Jesus!

To my dad: You will always be my greatest coach! Love you so much!

To Chris: Thank you for being the constant love and encouragement I have needed so many times. You are my husband, my best friend, and my leader. Like Jesus, you are humble enough to serve me and strong enough to lead me. I love you so much!

Preface

I have been a part of a coach's family my entire life, first as a coach's daughter and for the past 18 years, a coach's wife. There are some things people outside this coaching world need to know about what it's like living the lifestyle inside the coaching world. My fellow coaches' wives, this is for your entertainment and let you know you are not alone! Share this with others and read this devotion book for you!

1. Sports is our Livelihood, but it is NOT our Life.
Yes, sports is how we make a living, but we do not eat, sleep, breathe, or want to talk about it 24-7. It is always funny to me that people find the oddest times to talk about last night's, last week's, or last year's game: bathroom, church pew, vacation. Nobody, not even a coach, wants to talk about the fourth quarter play call while they are in the urinal. Sports is not our life, and it shouldn't be yours either!

2. A coach's family makes time sacrifices for team success.
My husband loves this game and works so freaking hard at being the best he can be so that the team can be the best they can be. Watching film on weekends and four nights a week at the field can lead to days the kids and I don't see our husband/dad. Yet, people can see him for two hours on a Friday night and complain publicly and have no idea what coaches sacrifice privately. Believe it or not…they want to win more than you do!

3. My husband's job depends solely on what 14-18 year old kids decide to do.
My husband and his staff have to prepare 40 teenagers to play together as one unit despite what might be going on at home, in the classroom or with the girlfriend. I have people tell me all the time how frustrated they are with their moody teenagers because they can't get their one kid to clean their rooms, be respectful or come home at curfew. Yet we expect coaches, somehow, to get perfection out of these teenagers on the field. It really should be considered

more of miracle working than coaching.

4. Coach's job is to focus on the team not an individual.
As a parent myself, I completely understand the love for your children. And, as parents our job is to watch, cheer, and encourage our kid. But the quickest way to bring down a team is focus on one individual, even if it's your wonderful, needs the ball every time, be the first 300-pound quarterback, child. You may not like every call the coaches make, but just know this: it's with the team, the whole team, in mind.

5. Coaching families don't have a lot of close friends.
Coaches have so many walls put up when it comes to relationships because people can't separate personal life from the professional one. We have to be guarded now because we have been burned before. People want to be friends until their child sits the bench. People want to be friends until their child gets disciplined. People want to be friends until we aren't winning anymore. Professional coaching can lead to personal loneliness.

6. Coaches are harder on themselves than you could ever be.
I have been around coaches my entire life, professionally and personally, and I have never met one that wasn't harder on themselves during a loss than anyone else. They stew over missed calls. They lose sleep over personnel changes. They watch play after play on film questioning what they could have done differently. There is no email, phone call, or personal attack that makes a coach think "oh, I hadn't thought about that, thanks for bringing that to my attention." I know what it *does* make them think, but I can't write that because we love Jesus.

7. My husband can't hear anything you say from the stands, but his family can.
There is a reason that my kids and I have had to move our seats so we can't hear what people say. I understand sports is an emotional game, but let's spread the emotion. If you are going to yell from the stands at my husband for a bad play call, I better hear you yell at your kid for missing the tackle, missed shot or dropped fly ball. We

are an equal opportunity team sport.

8. Coach's wives are the best secret keepers ever.
Whatever conversation you have with me in hopes I will share with my husband will NEVER get to him! The coach's wife is often treated like a side door into the coach's office. No, I don't know what my husband is going to do about playing time. No, I don't know how my husband is going to handle your child missing practice. No, I don't know why the freshmen are playing more than the upperclassmen. No, I don't know why parents aren't allowed in the locker room on game day. And guess what? I am not going to ask him either…he's not even going to know we had this conversation.

9. Coaching is a calling.
My husband makes $0.43 an hour for his coaching duties so we know he loves what he does because it's not for the money. As followers of Christ, our jobs are not given to us by man but by God. As coaches we may think athletic directors, parents, or administrators hold our jobs in the palms of their hands, but the truth is God in control of our path because we have submitted our calling. There are tough losses, tough seasons, and tough jobs. We may get fired from one but believe God will lead us to a different one. We know when things go well it's because of God, and when things go bad we will be okay because we have God.

10. Team is family and family is team.
We believe this with everything in us. This is why we call our family Team Roberts and why we believe the team is an extension of our family. We love these kids and know that our own children really have 40 big brothers. We view coaching as a calling and the team as a family. There are no two things that will put us on our knees in prayer more than football season and family. It is every coach's heaven that players, coaches, parents, and administration would work together to show love and respect to each other out of love and respect for God.

Foreword by Carol Stoops

University of Oklahoma

I love women's spirit, their heart, their strength! We are nurturers, we are care givers, and we are wives, sisters, daughters, and mothers. And like Sarah, some of us are a coach's wife. We know the importance of remaining steady in the storm for we are the rock in our household. Everyone looks to us to keep the world spinning in an orderly fashion. I don't know about you, but there are times when the world gets incredibly heavy on my shoulders and then I remember, I am not in charge of everything! He is! Whew…what a relief! I wish I remembered this on a moment to moment basis but I admit it; I need to be reminded. I'm guessing most coaches' wives (aka highly independent women) do, and what an incredible tool we have in *"Just Ask"* to guide us.

As a master story teller, Sarah draws you in with her heart and insight. Each devotional is based on the story of a Bible character and then Sarah pairs them with a coach's wife's testimony.

You will feel encouraged, empowered and refreshed….you know these women; you *are* this woman!

The stories will bless and comfort you with the "knowing" that we are all in this together. We are far more alike than different in what we go through. Although on different sides of the scoreboard, it is a fraternity, a sisterhood like no other. When we pray for each other, band together, and build one another up, this is how we come to a place of strength to be able to encourage our husbands. You know how the flight attendant instructs to put your oxygen mask on first before assisting others? This inspired collection of stories is the constant reminder that Jesus is our oxygen mask! They encourage us in our relationship with Him so we can show up fully present for our husband and our family.

I met Sarah for the first time at a bible study she was starting for the coaches' wives on our staff. I knew I had a friend forever! Not just a friend…a wise, relatable friend in whom I could trust and share without fear of judgment. She gets sports…as a woman, as a wife of a coach, and as a mother to children who participate… like all of us juggling all the those balls in the air! She is honest and real, sharing that life doesn't always look pretty for her either! I'm a true believer in "it takes a village," a village of girlfriends, coaches' wives, moms!

I love how she can make ancient scripture so real and like our stories today. She is a master story teller, always bringing it back to the real, the messy, and the funny. And finally how Jesus makes everything make sense and makes it all perfect…perfectly messy that is!

Sarah is a builder of people through her story telling and did just that for me. I wanted to write the *best* foreword for this unique and moving devotional and then insecurity snuck in so I voiced this to Sarah. Her quick response was a story from when we first met. She says I encouraged her, thus she was building me. She shared a verse she says to herself every time she writes or speaks, "Don't worry about what you will say or how you will say it, for it is not you who is speaking, but the Holy Spirit speaking through you." Matthew 10:19-20. Need I say more? And then she added Jesus' disciples were worried about spreading the good news and being arrested, the good news…I will not be arrested!

I have a love-hate relationship with the introspection at the end of the devotions. After reading one you think….yes, that's great, love that story, love the lesson, and then I move on! Why would I want to answer questions directly applying and personalizing it to me? You know the answer. The questions and suggestions at the end of each devotion makes us dive deep; it's not just surface level scripture and entertainment. Over time, I will read and re-read these stories, searching out specific entries depending on what's happening in my life, and I know I will see the growth in my journey by doing so.

Sarah makes me laugh and in doing so I learn so much in the simple moments, the stories, and the conversations. In her book, you will find a sisterhood like Dorothy and her ruby slippers; you always had it and just never knew! In many ways, coaches' lives and our families live parallel lives. Sarah understands this as she lives it, too. What a gift she gives all of us in telling Bible stories that never change, much like our stories where the name of the school, the mascot, the school colors could all be changed, yet the story remains the same.

May God continue to bless your journey and our families!

Carol Stoops

The one thing that stands between us and our greatest fear is our faith…

Just Ask Daniel

Read Daniel's Story: Daniel 6

My husband asked my son what his favorite thing about "mom" was. He replied, "She never worries." The Academy can present me with my award at any time because apparently I have been giving the performance of a lifetime. I can worry… a lot. As women of sports, we all can. We treat worry as if it's our spiritual gift more than a tactic of our opponent. When worry is a tactic of our opponent, his teammates are control and fear.

Daniel was a man who loved the Lord so much that he prayed three times a day. Unfortunately, due to some jealous teammates a law was passed saying nobody could pray to anyone besides the King for 30 days. Daniel could have just waited a month before he prayed again, *but his faith in the Lord was stronger than his fear of the world.* Daniel's relentless devotion to God and his prayer life led him into the den of hungry lions as punishment. The moment the stone was rolled in front of the den, Daniel knew the only thing standing between a great fear of dying at the mouth of these lions was the great faith he had in the great God he prayed to. I believe that although Daniel was in a lion's den, his fear and worry did not keep him from praying, but instead led him to it.

When we enter the life of a coaching family, there are times that feel like we are entering a lion's den. Our enemy may not look like a lion, but it can certainly act like one. Satan can use people to devour us with insults when we fail to produce a winning season or attack us with hurtful words if we do not play their child.

I love Daniel's reply. King Darius asked if he was still alive, *"Long live the King! My God sent his angel to shut the lion's mouths so that they would not hurt me, for I have been found innocent in his sight. And I have not wronged you, your Majesty." Daniel 6:21-22*

This same God that shut the lions' mouths for Daniel is the same God that can shut the lions' mouths for us.

Just Ask Kristi Malzahn

Auburn University Football

As a coach's wife, many times we find ourselves in a place where jealousy, instability, idolatry, and even a form of "captivity" can lead us into an insecure place, making us feel as if we are in a lions' den.

My husband, Gus, coached high school football for fifteen years. During this time, we faced several different "lions" which sought to devour our marriage, family, job and peace. It came in several forms such as jealousy, envy, and financial struggles. The ultimate "lion" was the constant fear of losing our job or our reputation.

After being a successful head coach for fourteen years, an opportunity arose to move into the college ranks, which brought different challenges. All of the sudden the "lions" were on a national stage. After a bit of success on the field for Gus, I was the one who ended up in a lions' den.

This event caused me to confront who I was in the Lord. In the world's view, I went from being the "good wife of a successful husband" to being the liability for the same husband. I was portrayed as everything negative you can possibly imagine. I questioned what God was doing. How could He allow this to pass through His hands and be okay with it? The Lord used this to begin the process of teaching me who I was in Him.

In Daniel 6:10, it says that when he heard the decree of the king, he went to his room to pray and he gave thanks. I believe this is the step I took which allowed the healing and growth to take place in me. The day everything happened, I went to my room, got on my knees and told the Lord, "I don't know why this is happening or what You are doing. I know You can stop all of this if You want to, but I trust You even if You don't. I trust You and thank You for what you are doing regardless of the pain or where it might lead."

I began to search for answers in the Scriptures. These are three things I have found to be helpful and true in the face of every crisis.

- Take every thought captive – literally, take it to the Lord and ask Him what He says about that thought. Philippians 4:8 Whatsoever is true, right, pure, lovely…think on these things.
- Be thankful and give Him praise in all things.
- Trust Him – He is faithful. Because He is always good and loves us dearly, He says in Romans 8:28-29 He is using all of this to our good and using it to change us to look more like Him.

I am continuously learning new things about who I am in the Lord; however, what He has shown me is that He placed us here and when he is ready for us to be somewhere different, we will go. The best part of this is I don't have to read the press or social media or even look at the win/loss column to find out who I am anymore!

Just Ask Me

1. What lions of fear and worry are you facing right now? Future? Parents? Job?

2. How does the story of Daniel encourage you today?

3. What does God want to teach you as you wait in your lion's den of fear?

"This is my command-be strong and courageous! Do not be afraid or discouraged. For the Lord your God is with you wherever you go."

Joshua 1:9

We are not called to look back, but to look up…

Just Ask Lot's Wife

Read Lot and his Wife's story: Genesis 19:1-29

Scoreboards and record books are things our husbands use in their professions, but they are also items we can use as wives in our marriages. We like to keep score of all the things we have done by ourselves. Because of us, bills got paid, kids got taken care of, and the lawn got mowed. We want our husbands to know our home scoreboard is 1052-7. We also keep great record books. In these books are everything we have ever done right for the family and everything our husbands have ever done wrong. Just to be clear, our record books do not keep our own wrong doings because let's not forget the scoreboard. Trust me, these scoreboards and record books can leave us resentful and bitter pillars of salt, just like Lot's wife.

As we read the story, we learn the towns of Sodom and Gomorrah were destroyed because they had become so full of evil and corruption. God was willing to save Lot and his family, however, because of Lot's faith. The angels told them before they left, *"Run for your lives! And don't look back…" (vs. 17)* Lot's wife looked back and was turned into a pillar of salt. Why did she look back? Why do we?

I have learned that when we look back, it's about us. When we look up, it is about God. Lot's wife had a hard time letting go of the past and became bitter salt, and if we do not look up to God for help, so will we.

First Peter 5:2-4 is a great encouragement and challenge to me when I want to throw a pity party because no one wants to actually throw me a real party for being awesome. "*Care for the flock that God has entrusted to you. Watch over it willingly, not grudgingly—not for what you will get out of it, but because you are eager to serve God. Don't lord it over the people assigned to your care, but lead them by your own example. And when the Great Shepherd appears you will receive a crown of never-ending glory and honor."* God knows how hard life, marriage, and motherhood can be, and looking in the past does not help, only looking up does!

Just Ask Kari Bollant

University Of Illinois Women's Basketball

*A*hh…scoreboards. I have been guilty of focusing on my husband's mistakes and keeping a negative running record, while looking at my own past in a positive light. As I read the verse from 1 Corinthians 13, "Love does not demand its own way. It is not irritated and it keeps no record of wrongs," it was another sweet reminder that God's word is living and active in my life, if I allow it to continually change me from the inside out. I will not soon forget the summer of 2000, when I asked the Lord to 'crush my pride.' Now that had to be with the Holy Spirit's leading because: A. Who in their right mind would ever ask the Lord to 'crush' anything? B. I certainly knew I could be prideful at times but I had no idea what I was asking. He began to show me my heart, and this was the first situation he used.

I was at a friend's pool swimming with my daughters, Abi (4) and Regan (1). It was time to clean up to leave and I thought Abi was with the other kids but she decided to help clean up the toys out of the pool and fell in. I dove in and grabbed her in seconds, which felt like hours. As I pulled her up, she screamed, "I drowned Mommy, I drowned!" It was instant relief to hear her sweet voice, but then I heard that still small voice reminding me, "You're not above anything." You see 'I' had been a lifeguard for 9 years. 'I' am safe around water. 'I' am not careless. Then the still small voice said, "If this would have happened to Matt (my sweet hubby), you would have crucified him." Later at home, I told Matt what had happened and as soon as I told him, he quickly said, "I'm glad that wasn't me!" Sadly, he knew how I would have treated him. Pride. What an ugly, ugly thing.

You see, Matt knew I had kept a negative scoreboard for him, though we never discussed it at the time. God has done a sweet work in my life; however, I can easily revert back if I am not careful. My husband and I have a great life together and we love each other very much, but it's not without its struggles. This year has been full and crazy. At times I have had the opportunity to tell him 'I told you so.' Sometimes I took the high road of grace and kept my mouth shut, and unfortunately, sometimes I shamelessly did not. There are also times I can feel like I'm doing everything on my own because he's busy; therefore, I should get an award for being super woman. How beautiful would it be if I just continued to let the word of God retrain my thinking so I kept a record of 'rights' instead of a record of wrongs? If I had even more grace for my husband than I had for myself—Lord, let it be.

Just Ask Me

1. Are you more likely to keep a record book or scorebook in your marriage?

2. How has you or your husband's past affected your present circumstances?

3. You are awesome!! Sometimes we just need to hear that. Write down a prayer thanking God for the family he has given you and the awesome opportunities to take care of them.

"...Love does not demand its own way.
It is not irritable, and it keeps no records of wrongs."
1 Corinthians 13:4

God will ask us to trust Him with our children…

Just Ask Mary and Joseph

Read Mary and Joseph's Story: Luke 1:26-38,
Matthew 1:18-24, John 19:16-27

As women, there is something we usually view as 'ours.' We may even view them as our most prized possession, our trophies: they are our children. Whether we are talking about our birth children or our husband's players, we work hard for our kids. We have prayed and provided for them. We have special plans in store for them. We take pride in the amazing little humans God has given us, but there will come a time when God, our Father, will ask us to trust Him with our children.

We always refer to Jesus as God's Son, but sometimes we forget He was the son of Mary and Joseph, as well. Mary was the one who gave birth to him. Joseph was the one who named him. Mary was the one who fed him. Joseph was the one who taught the carpentry skills. From the moment the angels appeared to both Mary and Joseph, they became parents. They were going to love this baby; they were going to play and wrestle with him because he was their son, their child, their little boy.

Eventually there came a point when they had to remind themselves that although God had entrusted them with this baby, then teenager, then adult man, that He in fact belonged to God

God has entrusted us with His babies, His little girls, His teenage sons and there will be stages of life when we are going to have to trust God with the children He has given us. Maybe your child is struggling in school right now; you can trust Your Father with your child. Maybe your child is going through some rebellion and you just don't understand; you can trust your Father with your child. Maybe, you lost your child to death; you can trust your Father has your child. After all, your Father is their Father! In life, and in death, Mary and Joseph trusted God with their son.

Mary and Joseph trusted their Father with their son from the cradle to the cross, and because they did, their son became their Savior.

Just Ask Christine Donovan

Oklahoma City Thunder Basketball

It was Halloween evening 2000. Where was God when I was nine months pregnant and stopped feeling our baby move? Where was God when I went to our doctor the following morning and there was no heartbeat? Where was God when I was induced to deliver our dead baby girl? Where was God during the funeral when we placed our baby in her grave?

At the time I didn't know where God was. I thought He was angry at me for all the things I had screwed up during my life. I didn't realize God was all around me during this tragic time of my life. God was in the room when I delivered baby Jacqueline. He was with the doctors, nurses and friends who came to support and help Billy and me through this sad time. He held us up when it was so hard to stand up by ourselves.

I learned to trust Jesus during this time and although my faith was tested, I believe my faith got me through this sad time. I trust God's plan for my life and although I don't always understand, I have confidence He is working on my behalf and I trust in His plan for me. After experiencing a still birth I have been able to help so many other women who have experienced the same thing and guide them from darkness back in to the light.

I trust that I will be reunited with my daughter Jacqueline again and that God is holding her in the palm of his hand.

Just Ask Me

1. What is the hardest part about trusting God with your children (or husband's team)?

2. In your stage of life how is God asking you to trust him with your (His) children? Tired? Rebellion? Losing season?

3. How does the story of Mary and Joseph, as parents, encourage you in parenting yours?

"For the word of the Lord holds true, and we can trust everything he does."
Psalms 33:4

God is God and we are not Him…

Just Ask Sarah

Read Sarah's Story: Genesis 15 & 16

Watching the games is actually one of the hardest parts for me as a coach's wife. What is fun and exciting to the fans can actually create a ball of nerves that keep me from eating before games and pacing during games. I can watch an entire season with my eyes covered because I can not control the outcome. Here in lies the problem—as women, we like to be in control.

God had made a promise to Abraham that he would have a son. God went so far as to say, *"Look up into the sky and count the stars if you can. That's how many descendants you will have!" Genesis 15:5.* But it was now the fourth quarter and they are well past the child-bearing age. Sarah and Abraham knew the promise from God, but this late in the game someone had to take control and it did not look like it was going to be God. Sarah says *"…The Lord has prevented me from having children. Go and sleep with my servant. Perhaps I can have children through her." Genesis 16:2.*

If you are thinking "this can not end well," it does not! Sarah's need to take control instead of trusting God led to the birth of a son named, Ishmael. Ishmael is the descendant of Mohammed and the Muslim religion, which has led to the long time war between the Jewish and Muslim nations.

When we try to take control and be God there are always consequences. It may not lead to years of wars like Sarah, but it may lead to a strained relationship with your child or husband, the loss of a job, or a lot of added stress. As followers of Christ, we are not called to control our lives but to give them to the one who lost His. Right before Jesus was arrested to be crucified, He prayed,*"Father, if you are willing, please take this cup of suffering away from me. Yet I want your will to be done, not mine."* Jesus did not want to suffer and die on the cross, but because He gave up control of His life, God saved ours.

Just Ask Carolyn Allen

Highland Park High School, Dallas, Texas

As a coaching family, we have lived in four different cities and eight different houses. After making the fifth move and two more rentals, I was in tears as I begged Randy to make an offer on a certain house. He reluctantly agreed, and we began the process of inspection.

The report came back; the foundation was bad. All the brick would be removed, the foundation corrected, and then all the brick would be put back on the house. "What?!" The children's Bible song started playing in my head, "the foolish man builds his house upon the sand . . . but a wise man builds his house upon a rock . . . ." It was foolish to buy a house that had a faulty foundation. Randy was wise, and I should have trusted his judgment. A month later we found a wonderful house and have lived in it for fourteen years now.

I thought back to the home I had grown up in—not the house, but the home. The home I grew up in had a mom and dad who showed me love but didn't show me God. When the storms of life came and our home's foundation was tested, it crumbled. Our home was broken and my parents divorced when I was six. Both remarried. In fact, my dad remarried four more times. I always had questions about who God is. What is His will for my life? When I stole some costume jewelry and didn't get caught, how could I get rid of the shame and guilt I felt?

At age sixteen, a cheerleader friend, Tranette, invited me to spend the night, and there in her room, she answered all those questions. She told me that Jesus is God's son, who took my sin and shame on himself on the cross. If I believed in him, I would be forgiven and live forever with God in heaven. Acts 16.31 says, "Believe in the Lord Jesus Christ and you shall be saved, you and your household." I prayed with Tranette that night. Jesus gave me the freedom and foundation I was searching for! We began reading the Bible together before school, and my life was on a new path. Only two short years later, it intersected with Randy Allen, when we were both counselors at a Christian camp called Kanakuk.

God called me to be Randy's wife—a life of moving and risk into the unknown. Like Sarah, the wife of Abraham, I questioned and doubted at times, but I always sensed God's will in each coaching job and move. Wherever the path led, our footing was sure because our home was built on the strong foundation of Jesus Christ. On Christ the solid rock I stand, all other ground is sinking sand, all other ground is sinking sand.

Shortly before my mother died, she prayed with me to believe in Jesus. I saw Him fulfill the promise of believe in the Lord Jesus Christ and you shall be saved, you and your household.

"By faith Abraham heard God's call to travel to a place he would one day receive as an inheritance; and he obeyed, not knowing where God's call would take him. By faith he journeyed to the land of the promise as a foreigner; he lived in tents, as did Isaac and Jacob, his fellow heirs to the promise because Abraham looked ahead to a city with foundations, a city laid out and built by God." Hebrews 11.8-10 (the Voice)

Just Ask Me

1. Describe a time you tried to take control of something and it didn't work out like you hoped.

2. In your life, what do you have a hard time letting God control? Why?

3. Write a personal prayer to God asking him to take control and help you when you want to take it back.

"The Lord isn't really being slow about his promise, as some people think. No, he is being patient for your sake. He does not want anyone to be destroyed, but wants everyone to repent."
2 Peter 3:9

We are one…

Just Ask Job and his Wife

Read Job's story: Job 1 and 2

I have lived in a coach's house my entire life. First as a coach's daughter and now as a coach's wife. I had always thought they would be similar experiences, but they are not! The ups and downs, the moving from place to place, the amount of time it takes away from the family…all of this is so much harder as a wife than it ever was as a child. God has used the life of a coach to teach me lessons about being the wife of one.

In the story of Job, we read how God allowed Satan to destroy everything that was a part of Job: his servants were killed, his donkeys were stolen, and all of his children died. As we feel the pain Job must have been going through, we come to *Job 1:9, "His wife said to him, 'Are you still trying to maintain your integrity? Curse God and die.' "*

I remember reading this and wondering why Job's wife did not die with the rest of the family. **Could it be that God does not view the wife as a part of Job's family but, rather as a part of the man himself?** Jesus says in *Matthew 19:4-6, "…at the beginning the Creator made them male and female, For this reason a man will leave his father and mother and be united to his wife, and the two will become one flesh. So they are no longer two, but one flesh. Therefore what God has joined together, let no one separate."*

Coaching is not simply what our husband does, but it is a part of who he is. It is how he shows his integrity, passion, and heart. We, as the wife, can either resent it or embrace it. We are one and because of this, I am not just married to a coach, but we are a coaching family. For so long, I felt like it was either football or family, but as I decided to jump on board with what my husband was doing, I have learned it is football **and** family! The team is a family, and our family is a team.

Ladies, let me be one to admit, marriage is hard and when you are a part of a coaching family, sometimes it can just seem impossible. God created marriage, and what He brought together, let no sport separate.

Just Ask Kelly Tadlock

Texas Tech Baseball

I met Tim our last year in college at Texas Tech, after he was done playing baseball. I never knew him as a college athlete. I never played a day of organized sports in my life, and I never personally knew anyone who was a coach. So to say I was a little naive when it came to the world of sports would be a HUGE understatement. After all, I grew up in the same town that my parents and their parents lived in. I just assumed I would have the same kind of life, deep roots and family always within a few miles. Boy was I wrong!

Our adventure of head coaching included moving into a 50 year-old apartment that was connected to the athletic dorm. There I was, pregnant and with a two year old little girl on my hip, moving into a dorm! We lived in that dorm almost three years. During that time, we saved enough money to build a house and when we moved in to that house, I remember waking up every morning, and saying, "Thank you God." I just KNEW this would be the house our kids would grow up in and we would grow old in. However, not even six months into that house, Tim was offered an assistant coaching position at the University of Oklahoma. I was devastated; he was elated. I just wanted roots, but he wanted opportunity and had bigger dreams.

We sold that little dream house we had built in Denison, and I dug up the roots I planted and we headed north to Norman, Oklahoma. While opportunity was knocking on Tim's door, heartache and sorrow were knocking on mine. The first couple of years there were the hardest. I was balancing my pride, joy and support for Tim and this wonderful opportunity before him against my deep sadness, mourning the loss of my dad, the loss our new home, the loss of my home state, and feeling so far away from my grieving mom. It was the darkest time in my life.

A friend sent me a card and reminded me about the story of Job, and she also mentioned something about the importance to "Bloom where you are planted." Between Job and her words to me, I eventually decided to bloom where I was planted and trust God more. Dig a little deeper for the faith I felt I was losing. I got busy doing what a coach's wife does: make friends, take the kids to church, volunteer at the kids elementary school, and join PTA. I was going to plant roots and bloom, even though by this time, in the back of my mind, I was afraid that there might still be another move in our future. I learned to lean into the pain, the uncertainty, and embraced the idea that *this* is what life looks like when you are married to a coach.

I thank God every day for all He has taken away from me. I thank Him for the pain I have endured and for the healing that came in His time. I thank Him for showing me that while the dream I had for my life was a good one, He had a better one in mind. Now that we are in Lubbock, I can say, "Thank you God." Even though I hope our roots will be permanent ones in Lubbock, I know now that if we ever face another time in our lives when we are losing, whether it be a losing season, or losing loved ones or the place we call home, I never have to look any further than God's word to be reminded and reassured. There is always hope, and there is always another season of life to be lived.

Just Ask Me

1. Talk about a time when your sport has come between you and your husband.

2. I learned I can either be a bitter wife or a better family. What is one thing you can do as a wife to make your coaching family better? Go to games? Pray for daddy when he is gone? Have the players over?

3. So often we want to change our husband without going to the one who created him. As the *Power of a Praying Wife* book says… shut up and pray. Wife Challenge: Write down a prayer for your husband every day for the next 21 days.

"Always be joyful. Never stop praying. Be thankful in all circumstances, for this is God's will for you who belong to Christ Jesus."
1 Thessalonians 5:16-17

There is a time and season for everything...

Just Ask Esther

Read Esther's Story: Esther 1-7

As a coaching family, there will inevitably be a time when you will ask God, "Why do you have us here"? or "Why are you sending us there"? Reasons for these questions may include being fired, struggling with the coaching staff, parents, and/or motivation of the players. Often God uses seasons of preparation to ready us for seasons of revelation. There are no wasted struggles. There are no wasted tears. There are no wasted seasons.

Esther learned this lesson of God's timing and preparation when her people were on the verge of getting eliminated by the King's evil sidekick, Haman. Esther, a Jew, was made Queen of Persia. After learning of Haman's plan to exterminate the entire Jewish community, Esther's cousin pleaded with her to use her position as Queen to save their people. He beseeched her, *"Who knows, if perhaps you were made queen for just such a time as this?" Esther 4:14*

The Bible teaches us in *Ecclesiastes 3:1, "For everything there is a season, a time for every activity under heaven."* There was a season of preparation for Esther, a time to prepare her heart, mind, and body to become Queen of Persia. Then there was what all the preparation led up to, a time for her to use her position as queen to save her Jewish people. Just like the sports profession, God has a plan, a purpose, and a season for everything we do.

- A time to prepare and a time to play
- A time to plant and a time to harvest
- A time to hurt and a time to heal

I do not know what season of life you are in right now; it may be good, or it may be a struggle. You may be in a season of waiting, wondering, or wishing God would show himself. I want to encourage you that while you are waiting, God is working. While you are preparing, God is planning. Find hope and encouragement in the story of Esther for God is preparing you and your family for "such a time as this."

Just Ask Rachel Ruth Wright

Cardinal Gibbons High School Raleigh, North Carolina

*M*y husband, Steven, and I just celebrated our nineteenth wedding anniversary. Out of necessity, our celebration was several days before the nineteenth because it is football season, and he's the head coach of a high school team! Extra time, even for a significant milestone, is non-existent!

While I love the sports world and all that Steven does, I have discovered marriage is a greater challenge than the strongest opposing team. Marriage has not been easy for either of us. At times I feel as if I am running my twentieth "suicide" at the end of a long basketball practice—exhausted, in pain, and feeling like, can I even do this? Of course, not every day is bad. We have had plenty of laughter, precious memories and promises from the Lord to lean on. But I want to address the coach's wife who might be in a desperate marital situation.

When I have needed answers, I have gone to God's Word. I want to share some things God has taught me from the book of Esther.

Esther was in a desperate situation. Wicked Haman was plotting to kill the Jews, herself included. She knew she was going to have to go before the king, her husband, or she and her people would die. No small task, because if the king refused her approach to the throne, she would be immediately executed! With prayer and fasting she approached the throne. Esther was obedient to God's leading in her life, even if it meant her death. The king graciously received her and agreed to her request! God then used Esther to save the Jews and help bring about Haman's destruction. Like Esther, do you find yourself in a desperate situation? Your adversary—Haman—is the enemy, the devil. He is plotting the destruction of your marriage. The enemy's strategy to destroy your marriage is multi-faceted. He will attack the finances, remove family time due to a busy coach's schedule, allow past pains or abuses to resurface and cause estrangement, present subtle sexual temptations that can lead to marital destruction, allow small hurts to build until they fester over the years…the list goes on.

But you and I can be an Esther! As coaches wives, we have to be tougher than ten defensive lines put together. God allows us to go through difficulties in marriage to draw us to His throne. Just like Esther brought her request to the king, we can bring our requests for our marriage to the King of kings! Praise God! He doesn't ever turn us away. He will lovingly listen to all you have to say, then guide and lead you through His Word. So you must—this isn't an option—you must be in God's Word every day! What I am continually learning is that when I am in His word, my focus is on my King instead of my marriage, and I am helped.

Like Esther, you may think you or your marriage will die, but in the end, God's plan for you, as it was for Esther, will be better then anything you could imagine! So…bring your marriage before than King! He will receive you and help you. Trust Him with the outcome. Just trust Him!

Just Ask Me

1. What season of life would you say you are in right now? Waiting? Harvest? Planting?

2. Describe a season in your life where you saw God preparing you for something with purpose?

3. Pray and ask God what He wants to teach you using the story of Esther.

"Yet God has made everything beautiful for its own time."
Ecclesiastes 3:11

There is no gift or talent that is insignificant…

Just Ask the Boy

Read The boy's story: Matthew 14:13-21

I once was asked, "If you won the lottery, how would you spend the money?" My response then is the same now—pay someone to make my kids' lunches. Lunches are my nemesis. How important could a lunch be?

Pretty important a few thousand years ago.

A little boy left his house one morning with a simple lunch his mom had packed for him, something that just seemed insignificant and ordinary. That day, the boy was going to listen to a teacher named Jesus along with a crowd of an estimated 25,000 people. Jesus asked his disciples what food they had to feed the people. They pointed to this little boy who had his lunch: two fish and five loaves of bread. Jesus told them to bring Him what they had and watch Him work. He wants to do the same for you and me. To the boy, to the people, and to the disciples, what the boy had to offer seemed insignificant. Gifts in the hands of man can be insignificant, but gifts in the hands of God can change the world.

We have all been given gifts and talents by God to be used for God. Yes, You! We can struggle seeing the significance in the ordinary, especially when others around us seem to have gifts that appear bigger and better.

Comparison kills our contentment. Do you see how a friend makes meals for all the players and you burn toast? Do you see how cute another wife always looks and you are lucky if you get out of your sweat pants. Do you find yourself saying "I'm just a mom." We are all standing in front of Jesus with our two fish and five loaves saying "This is all I've got." Jesus, will in turn, say, "This is all I need."

Jesus just needs all we've got! The little boy could have kept at least one fish or one loaf for himself, just to be safe. We will all be tempted to hold back from God too: our fears, our past, our insecurities, our hearts… just to be safe. The problem with safe is that it only feeds one.

Just Ask Jill Freeze

Ole Miss Football

*D*isconnected is the best word I could use to describe how I was feeling after Hugh took over as the head football coach at Arkansas State University. During his previous tenure as a position coach, the smaller number players he led afforded me the opportunity to invest alongside of him. However, as his position in leadership grew, I did not know how I could practically make a difference with the whole football team. I started asking God to show me how I could be a part of the story he was writing with our lives.

At first, I did not like the answer God gave me, which was to lead a Bible study with the other coaches' wives. I reminded God of the many reasons why this would not work. "They aren't all Christians, we are from many different denominations. I work full time already, I have three active children. I won't have time to prepare. Others are more qualified than I am…I am not enough."

God did not let up on His calling of me. I attempted partial obedience, a Bible study taught by video. Halfway through the study I knew this was not working. Finally, I surrendered. I told the wives that we were starting a new study called "*The Coach's Wife,*" and I was going to teach it. The first week nine wives showed up and literally sobbed throughout the entire meeting while repeatedly saying, "I can't do this." But the next week an amazing thing occurred; they all came back. Six years later, God has been faithful! Now at Ole Miss, our group has grown to 23 faithful members.

In spite of me, God has been at work! The story that He continues to write is sweeter than I could have ever dreamed. A closeness has developed among us that has formed such a strong bond. Marriages have been strengthened through the support, prayer, love and service we extend to each other, and the sacrifices required for this job are easier to make since we are so invested in each other and in the team through prayer cards we send to each player each week of the season. Best of all, more of my football family have come to know Jesus as their personal Lord and Savior.

God has been faithful to multiply the minutes in my days to give me time to study and prepare. He has grown my thirst for His Word, as I am continually faced with tough questions from the wives that only He can answer. Out of our group, he has birthed another Bible study to include the wives from other sports and administration positions within our program. God has more than doubled the number of women for me to teach.

My nerves still get the best of me, but I am excited about being connected to the story God is writing with our family!

Just Ask Me

1. Comparing ourselves to others often keeps us from pursuing God and his personal plans for us. How has comparison kept you from being content with who God made you?

2. As Christians, God gives each one of us gifts to use on our teams and in our life. Read 2 Corinthians 12:12-30. How do the gifts God has given each of us work according to this passage?

3. Identify some actual steps you need to take in order to "Bring" your gifts to Jesus. Pray about it? Talk to someone? Make an action plan?

"All of you together are Christ's body, and each of you is a part of it."
1 Corinthians 12:27

Winning our battles means focusing on what God says not what we see...

Just Ask the Israelites

Read the Israelites story: Numbers 13 &14

Two of the biggest fears women have are the fear of being alone and the fear of failure. When you put these two fears together and pair them with the lifestyle of sports, as coaches wives we can live in fear a lot. Due to the demands of the job, we may spend a lot of time alone, physically and emotionally. During the season, we can find ourselves being both mom and dad, mowing the grass, and even trying, often unsuccessfully, to fix the plumbing! These fears can force us into hiding from the world instead of facing our fears and finding God.

In this story, God sent the Israelites to fight a giant enemy in order to take over the land. This was land God said He was giving to the Israelites. God promised them a victory, yet they never got to experience it because they chose to focus on what they saw instead of what God said. They focused on their fears instead of their faith. What could giants do when you have God telling you, "I am giving you this land?" It sounds crazy, but we allow doubt and fear to take over just like the Israelites.

Jesus said, "I have come so that you may have life and have it to the full." (John 10:10) That is our promised land, life to the fullest, more than we can ever imagine. But then we see the giants: fear, depression, discouragement, failure and thoughts of inadequacy.

We focus on giant after giant, fear after fear, failure after failure. These giants are keeping us from entering the promised land of life to the full. Ladies, it is time to listen to our head coach's words! Jesus said *"In this world you will have trouble. But take heart! I have overcome the world." John 16:33*

We will all face giants, but when we believe who God is, we will become who God says we are—giant killers!

Just Ask Abbie McCoy

University of Maryland Wrestling

*D*uring my adventures as the wife of a coach, I grapple with multiple giants on a daily basis, and I understand now that they all stem from my fear of failure. I fear I will not be able to provide enough for my children and that I can't be all they need when my coach is on the road.

One of the biggest giants I have faced since having children is that of inadequacy. Since my husband is out of town a lot, I feel inadequate and afraid that I can't possibly be all my children need in their lives. The more inadequate I allow myself to feel, the more the other giants creep in and create unneeded stress on my life and my relationship with my husband. Because I felt like I needed to be everything for my kids, I was feeling so overwhelmed that I was having trouble even doing the small things. The more I focused on how many times he came home late or couldn't be there for something, the more depressed I became and the less I enjoyed the blessings.

One day I was complaining to a good friend, who is a pastor's wife, about my frustrations with my coach's schedule. She listened and then told me I was lying to myself. I was a bit shocked at first, but she continued and reminded me that Satan wants us to lie to ourselves. He wants us to believe we are failures, that we are inadequate, that our husbands aren't around enough or that somehow our children won't have the perfect upbringing we dreamed of when they were first born. These lies lead to giants who take over our thoughts and happiness.

Now when I start to listen to the lies in my head and hear the rumble of giants creeping up on me, I pray for Jesus to silence the lies by remembering all the blessings that go along with being a coach's family. By focusing on the positive, God allows me to enjoy even the lonelier moments. I realize God has provided me with a husband who is a positive role model for our family by selflessly caring so much for others and that the people he brings in our lives bless our family. During the lonely times, I give myself a break and realize I can't do it all; my kids will be ok if we skip an event that I am too tired to go to by myself. It was only when I started looking at my unique situation as a blessing did I understand the joy my life could bring me. When I pray to silence the giants and focus on the blessings is when I really start to feel like my husband's career has given my family more than I can imagine. We have an extensive network of athletes and coaches who bless our lives and are a positive example for my kids, we have traveled to amazing places, and the positive role models they meet uplift us all.

Just Ask Me

1. What is the biggest "giant" you face on a daily basis as a wife, mom, woman?

2. How do giants keep you from living a full life with Jesus, your promised land?

3. Look in God's Word for the promises that will defeat these giants and write down these verses on note cards as reminders.

"Let us then approach God's throne of grace with confidence, so that we may receive mercy and find grace to help us in our time of need."
Hebrews 4:16

You can be led by the Holy Spirit into the wilderness…

Just Ask Jesus

Read Jesus' story in the wilderness: Matthew 4:1-11

When living in a sports family, we all encounter the, no-fun, losing seasons, but there are also those devastating losing seasons of life that can bring us to our knees in tears because our hearts are shattered. The wilderness of brokenness due to a strong-willed child, the death of a parent, or a struggling marriage. Whether you are facing losing seasons in sports or life, each one can make us doubt where God is and lead us to ask God some hard questions. Why us? What did we do wrong?

Let the story of Jesus being led into the wilderness encourage you as you walk through yours. The Bible says in *Matthew 4:1, "Then Jesus was led by the Spirit into the wilderness to be tempted there by the devil. For forty days and forty nights he fasted and became very hungry."* Jesus did nothing wrong yet found himself in a wilderness alone, hungry, and facing temptations from his enemy. We learn that God allows us to face trials, not because we have done anything wrong, but to show us His ways are always right. Jesus says in *John 5:17 "My Father is always working, and so am I." We can ask God "What are you doing?" and His answer will always be "I am working."*

During these times God may not be building our careers, but our character. He may not be seen, but He can be trusted. It may seem things are really bad, but when you are doing life with Jesus He will show you that He is still good. Doing life with Jesus doesn't mean the end of problems; it means the end of facing problems alone. Jesus says in *John 16:33, "I have told you all this so that you may have peace in me. Here on earth you will have many trials and sorrows, but take heart because I have overcome the world."* Remember, God is not interested in growing our fans; instead He wants to grow His followers. He is not just interested in keeping us happy; He wants to make us holy, and sometimes that means allowing us to enter into and out of some losing seasons.

Just Ask Juli Boeheim

Syracuse University Basketball

Growing each season brings with it many highs and lows. I have noticed that even after coaching for 40 years, it's only the losses that my husband really responds to, much like a temporary death (as he has described it). The wins are what is expected, nothing to get too crazy about…. it's on to the next game so no time for celebrating.

The onset of the basketball season is such an exciting time in our lives, lots of unknowns and the sky is the limit! Clear blue skies. I love all that comes with that first day of practice and could stay in that sunshine mode indefinitely. The games do seem to change the pulse a bit, and for many seasons, that's when the dreaded storm winds start swirling. We can lock our windows and doors, but it's inevitable; eventually the storm barges in. It hovers in the family room and sits with us at our dining table for the duration of the season. It affects every aspect of our lives and our home.

Over the years, I have learned that the storms will come, both on and off the court. However, knowing who is in control of every circumstance in our lives at all times provides an anchor for emotions, fears, and the "what ifs." It is in those very storms that God does some of His greatest work in us. We have been hit with some hurricanes, tornadoes, blizzards of late, and those are the doozies that challenge us on every level. We have found ourselves being loyal to those we believe in and count as family with repercussions to follow, as well as questioning justice and the fairness of the process. However, we cannot question God and have refused to go there. In the midst of our on-the-court storms, we have also suffered the loss of both of my parents in less than nine months. That is something I could never have imagined.

God holds it all. Period. He really does. And although I have had my moments, I have learned to look for His Almighty fingerprints on every single thing. I can now so clearly see His blessings when the walls seem to be crumbling down around us in the midst of the cyclone. He knows the end even from the beginning of each storm. He writes powerful scripts that change lives with His exclamation point! The 2015-2016 season was a prime example. We started the season with NCAA investigations and sanctions and yet the season ended with our team, a bubble team, playing in the Final Four! As I have said publicly, only God could write this script, and He will have the final say on our program and our lives! I am so thankful for the hope God gives us on a dark, stormy and desolate day. The sun will come out again!

Just Ask Me

1. Describe a time God has led you into a wilderness. Tough season. Life struggle.

2. Realistically, how do you view God when you face a struggle in your life? Helper? Punisher? Distant?

3. How does Jesus' story in the wilderness encourage your faith?

"So do not fear, for I am with you; do not be dismayed, for I am your God. I will strengthen you and help you; I will uphold you with my righteous right hand."
Isaiah 41:10

Sometimes the greatest thing to do for our family is to be with our Jesus…

Just Ask The Disciples

Read the Disciples story: Mark 6:30-32

Something you need to know about me is I have run out of gas so many times it's ridiculous. I don't mean I have coasted into the gas station on fumes. I mean, stopped in the middle of the road with my hazard lights on out of gas as people tell me they are my #1 fan. My thoughts are, "I can do one more thing. I don't have time to stop." But then I find myself unable to do anything for anyone because I am stuck on the road. If we don't put gas in the tank, the car is useless in its purpose. SO ARE WE.

One of the greatest definitions of sacrifice I have heard is "giving up something you love for something you love even more." As women, wives, and moms, we sacrifice much because we love many. We are mom, wife, counselor, friend, taxi-driver and much more. Our lives are busy and overwhelming. We may find ourselves hiding in the closet, all because we have let our gas tank run empty. Jesus understood it, lived it, and shows us how to handle it.

We read in this story that the disciples were coming and going; so many people, so many needs, no time to stop and eat. Does that sound familiar? We make sure everyone is taken care of first, before we think about ourselves. There is a problem in all the sacrifice; at some point we will get burned out because our gas has run out. Once we are burned out, resentment can set in. We can become resentful toward our family, friends, or co-workers because we feel nobody understands. The truth is Jesus understands.

Jesus says in the very next verse, "*Come with me by yourselves to a quiet place and get some rest.*"

The problem is we think rest is simply getting away. But Jesus knew rest doesn't just come in a vacation; it comes in a person, by getting alone with Him. We need to fill up our whole gas tank and that means both physically and spiritually. So put down this book, spend some time in prayer, and book a vacation!

Just Ask Donna Smith

University of Memphis Basketball

I have been married to Tubby for more than 40 years now. As a coach's wife, mom, and grandma, life can get so focused on others that we forget to take care of ourselves. As a coach's wife, you can be the one that handles a lot of the day to day home activities by yourself. When Tubby was hired as the Head Coach for the University of Memphis in April 2016, he immediately left our home in Lubbock, Texas to start his new job in Memphis, Tennessee. It was my responsibility to sell the house, pack the house, and move the house. It was exhausting. We do it because we love our husbands and our families, but we have to remember to take care of ourselves while we are taking care of others.

I really connected with the story of Jesus and the disciples because it stressed to me the importance of taking care of ourselves in the midst of dealing with loved ones, players and staff, kids, grandkids, moving etc. If we don't treat ourselves every now and then, then we are not any good to others. The Bible says our bodies are like temples; we must not let it go. The old saying, "Use it or lose it" is very true.

We all need a break from the monotony. We all need a break from the mundane. We need to decompress, pray, and meditate so we can have peace during these times. Many times I would hide in the bathroom to pray and meditate. I just needed Jesus to fill me up so I could pour out to others. If only for a short time, it would be a respite from the rigors of life stuff.

Whatever adventures this life as a coaching family gives us, we have to always remember that getting alone by ourselves with God to take care of ourselves is the best thing we can do for our family. Whether we are in Kentucky, Texas, or Tennessee, this is a lesson I take with me wherever God leads us.

Just Ask Me

1. Realistically, what are some things you do when you get tired and overwhelmed? Nap? Social Media? Read?

2. Write about a time you have been bitter because you have been burned out?

3. What keeps you from getting alone with God daily?

4. How does the story of the disciples and Jesus encourage you?

"Then Jesus said, 'Come to me, all of you who are weary and carry heavy burdens, and I will give you rest.'"

Matthew 11:28

It is impossible to win the battle if we are fighting the wrong enemy…

Just Ask John the Baptist

Read John the Baptist's story: John 3:22-36

There always seems to be a transition periods at both the beginning and ending of each season. In the beginning, it is hard because we love having our coach around, and now our kids have to share him with the players (his other kids). At the end, it is equally hard because the kids and I are used to how things are going and have found our rhythm. With each transition, tensions can arise. We can see his professional success and feel our personal loneliness. We have to remember, we have any enemy but it is not our husband.

John was a man of God who taught repentance and baptized people when they came back to God. When it came time for Jesus to show the world He was the Messiah, He asked John to baptize him. One day John's friends came to him and said, *"Rabbi, the man you met on the other side of the Jordan River, the one you identified as the Messiah, is also baptizing people. And everybody is going to him instead of coming to us." (John 3:26)* John's friends were actually upset that people were getting baptized by God himself and not them.

Believe me, we can all get caught up in the "what about me?" Our enemy wants nothing more than for us to die to this disease, but God calls us to die to self. I love John's response to his disciples… "I am filled with joy at his success. He must become greater and greater, and I must become less and less." (John 3:29b).

John was so confident with his role on the team that he was filled with joy at someone else's success. John knew the battle was not with Jesus, but against the enemy who wants us to keep the focus on ourselves and because Jesus was his focus, his personal needs were met. Sweet girl, your needs are met because of Christ and Christ alone. As a coaching family, God puts us all in our roles during each season, so He can have joy at our success!

Just Ask Amy Yousey

Oklahoma Baptist University Soccer

When I first met my husband, twenty-plus years ago, he was already a soccer coach at the age of 16. As we fell deeper in love and set our life goals I thought "how fun" it would be to be a coach's wife. You would see a coach's wife on TV and see them looking all cute and happy; little did I know then how hard it would really be. Being a coach's wife is full of everyday battles. I will not lie, I have fallen many times. You have to have a lot of patience and most of all a lot of FAITH in the Lord. There are times I have found myself thinking, "Why did I believe this life would be fun?" The late nights and constant schedule changes can really wear you out, especially when trying to schedule your own family events. Being married to a coach you have to be able to have tough skin and know not everyone is going to say nice things about your spouse. Many times I have had to bite my tongue. You also have to realize that his team is like his family, and many times they may come before you. This is where I struggle most.

There was a time after my youngest was born, when my husband had to be gone for Labor Day weekend for a couple of his competitive teams. I remember being home alone with our one month old and our toddler. It was so hard; both kids would cry and I was so overwhelmed with it all. I called my husband and said "I just can't take this anymore I want a divorce; you left me home alone with our children and put your team before us all the time" and then hung up on him. He called me right back and said "I am coming home, I will call the director now and tell him I quit. You and the boys are more important to me then anything else." Right then I knew I wasn't being fair to him and I needed to change myself. Of course it didn't help I was having some postpartum depression issues.

Prayer is what helps me get through those tough times. Our family quote is "I can do all things through Christ who strengthens me" Philippians 4:13. My husband is a godly man and a dedicated, loving, and intelligent soccer coach. He has worn many hats as a coach: a teacher, a mentor, a friend, a brother, a father, a spiritual leader, and a role model. I see the joy and love in his eyes when he is out there with any of his soccer teams; I would never ask him to give that up. I am his number one fan. The best advice I can give to other coaches wives is to pray daily and make friends with the other wives because they, too know how tough it can be.

Remember that God chose you to be a coach's wife so you must be better at it than you think. "A worthy wife is her husband's joy and crown…"

Just Ask Me

1. What are your family's season transition periods like?

2. How does John's attitude toward his disciples encourage you?

3. Read Ephesians 6:11-18…How does God want you to apply this to the battles we face as a coaching family?

"You will keep in perfect peace all who trust in you,
all whose thoughts are fixed on you!"
Isaiah 26:3

It is impossible for someone, other than Jesus, to meet our needs…

Just Ask the Samaritan Woman

Read the Samaritan woman's story: John 4:3-26

From the moment we are born, we are given the desire to be loved and accepted in this world. It is the reason we are tempted to buy the newest car, house or clothes, just to fit in. Although we put on different masks to fit in and feel accepted, we really long for people to look at us and really see us for who we are, not what we pretend to be. Unfortunately, we often seek this from everybody except Jesus, much like the Samaritan woman.

The Samaritans were a group of people who were considered outcasts, people the Jews avoided. In the story, a Samaritan woman had come to draw water from the well, in the middle of the day, when most other women would come early in the morning. She was an outcast among outcasts. Why? We know she had been married five different times and the man she was currently living with was not her husband. She was looking for love and acceptance in all the wrong places, but then she met Jesus. Jesus saw her and showed love to her. In Jesus, she found what she had been looking for in the world: love for her heart, healing from her past, and purpose for her future.

The woman left her water jug at the well, rushing back into town telling those who had rejected her about Jesus. She forgot who she was because she found who she wanted to be—a woman of worth. She was no longer hurt by the rejection she received from the world because she had found acceptance in the One who created the world. The Samaritan Woman came to the well to get drinking water but found living water. She came to the well, lost but left found. She came to the well by herself but left with a Savior.

Like the Samaritan woman, we search the world for what Jesus died to give us: love, acceptance, and hope. Although we have no idea what her name was, I do know what it could have been: mine or yours. Jesus saw this woman's heart, and He is wanting to reach out to each of ours.

Just Ask Amber Wright

Retired Buffalo Bills, Ft. Gibson High School

I feel like I can completely relate to the Samaritan woman's story. As a young girl thousands of miles from home and newly married, I was her. In our second year of marriage, Kenyatta and I moved to Orchard Park, New York. We lived there for three years while he played football for the Buffalo Bills. My days were spent chasing a toddler, calling my mom and counting the hours until Kenyatta walked through the door. I also spent days being painfully insecure, feeling like I wasn't enough. I now know that I am not enough and am completely okay with that. God's grace is enough!

I often met him at the door with the day's disappointments and my expectations. Sometimes verbally, other times in silence waiting for him to figure it out. He never figured it out. He wasn't meant to; he would have never. I promise he could have given me the world and I would have still needed more. I did need more; I needed to wholly surrender to the one that created me. Expectations in relationships often lead to disappointment. I expected him to notice when I cleaned the house or did the laundry. Not only notice, but thank me, get me flowers, and celebrate my accomplishments. That is a big deal! My unrealistic expectations were that my husband and my marriage would satisfy my soul. My soul is created to be satisfied, but satisfied by no one but my Savior. I searched, I expected, I demanded and yet nothing satisfied. Freedom came when I finally understood that my fulfillment could not come from my relationship with Kenyatta, but only through my relationship with my God who loves me. Oh, what an amazing freedom it is. I thank God daily for His grace that has sustained our marriage for 17 years. By His grace alone.

Just Ask Me

1. Like the Samaritan woman, who are you looking to in order to meet your needs? Husband? Kids? Friends?

2. In what areas do you feel you look to others for acceptance? Emotionally? Mentally? Spiritually? Why?

3. Write a prayer asking Jesus to meet you at your well.

"I have come so that you may have life and have it to the full."
John 10:10

When we give our life to Jesus, it doesn't mean the end of problems, it means the end of facing problems alone…

Just ask Paul and Silas

Read Paul and Silas' story: Acts 16:16-40.

I have nicknames for each of my kids. My daughter, Chloe, and I were talking about each one: C: "Why do you call Cale your heart?" Me: "Because he is the one that made me a mom" C: "Well, I am the one who makes you a hard-working mom."

Do you have those people in your life that make you a hard-working Christian? They are just not easy to love sometimes. It could be a fan in the stands, your mother, a parent, a child, or another coach's wife. We all have these people! How do we deal with them?

In the story, we learn Paul and Silas were beaten, mocked and put in prison by people who didn't agree with their faith. While in prison, they began praying and singing hymns for all to hear. There was an earthquake, and all the doors flew open and the chains were broken.

The jailer, who most likely took part in the beatings, was about to kill himself when Paul stopped him and assured him, the prisoners were all there. The jailer said, *"Sirs, what must I do to be saved?" Acts 16:29*

I know you are thinking, "There is no way in the world I can start singing hymns and praying with these people." I get it. The answer is not what they did, but who their focus was on. It was not on the jailer who locked them up; it was on Jesus who could set them free. They were not focused on the negative words of the world but on the true words of Jesus. They were not focused on their pain physically but on the one that saved them spiritually. They were not focused on the enemy that put them there but the God that could get them out.

This story shows us what faith in the one true God can look like, and what can happen when our faith is put into action. We get to rejoice because what the enemy uses to drive us over the edge is what God uses to make lost people found.

Just Ask Sherri Riffe

Retired High School Girls Basketball

*T*he year was 1981. After saying "I will never coach girls," my husband was offered and accepted the head girls basketball/track coaching position at our local high school. In spite of a 1-19 record, this first year was a great experience, and his love for coaching girls was evident! Two years later, he became the huddle leader for the Fellowship of Christian Athletes in the school and was excited to see these girls grow to love Jesus through FCA.

We have three daughters and since 1981, we have had 15-20 "adopted" daughters per year whom we considered part of our family. We enjoyed hosting team dinners, helping financially if it was needed, giving rides home from games etc.

Fast forward to 1990. Everyone was enjoying success on the court and track. Our three daughters were now playing; life was good! THEN CAME THE CALL. Coach was told he needed to be at the school board meeting Tuesday evening and there would be a group of upset parents who wanted him fired! I could come, but no students were allowed at the meeting.

As we entered the room, Christ's crucifixion came to my mind... was this how Jesus felt when the angry mob gathered before him? The room was separated into two sections: seats on the west were "against the coach" and seats on the east were "for the coach."

So many hard feelings were taking over my thoughts. Memories of the past nine years of my husband's coaching career were going through my mind. Time and energy spent with the girls on the teams he coached, fixing and sharing meals, hugs to celebrate wins or console losses, the Christian role model he had been to these parent's daughters…and now this?! How dare they?!

At seven o'clock the meeting began. There would be five parents "against the coach" speaking and five parents "for the Coach" speaking. A five-minute timer was set by the board president. As the first speaker continuously shuffled papers on the podium the timer went off. The next four speakers could not collect their thoughts enough to express their concerns about Coach and the time would ring before they were finished speaking. Could God shuffle those papers and scramble their thoughts so they could not speak words against Coach? "For the coach" speakers were next and they were articulate in their speeches, with words of thanks, appreciation, encouragement, and love toward Coach and our family. I knew at that moment, like Paul and Silas, Jesus was in that room just like he was in that jail. Everything was going to be OK! They voted 5-0 to keep our coach…Praise God!

Forgiveness does not change the past, but it does change the future! Fast forward, coach is retired, and our daughters are grown with families and careers. We still live in the same community with the same people. I am so thankful to Jesus for His Word, that forgiveness is essential, not easy, but effective! I know Jesus loves and forgives me therefore, I, too, needed to forgive the "against coach" parents. I was encouraged by *2 Chronicles 20:15, "for the battle is not yours, but God's."*

Just Ask Me

1. How does the story of Paul and Silas' joy and compassion for the jailer encourage you today?

2. Write down the names of those difficult people in your lives (use code if needed).

3. With the help of Jesus, write down a prayer for each one.

"The foolish plan of God is wiser than the wisest of human plans, and God's weakness is stronger than the greatest of human strength."

1 Corinthians 1: 25

When you feel overlooked by people, you are being seen by God...

Just Ask David

Read David's Story: 1 Samuel 16: 1-1

It was game day. A day that meant rushing everyone home from school to change clothes, grab some sandwiches and be on our way to watch our favorite coach. But of course, everyone wanted to fight over spit bubbles, music, and the imaginary lines in the seats. About 30 minutes into the trip, I couldn't take it any more and I did what every parent threatens to do—I pulled the car over. These words came from my mouth: "For the rest of the trip everyone is going to pray that their future wife/husband loves Jesus because it is times like these that one parent keeps the other parent from killing the kids. And dad isn't around right now so you will be lucky to make it through this season alive."

As coaches wives, we can often have the following thoughts:

"Does anyone know all the things I do for my family?"

"Does anyone know what it takes to keep a family going during my husband's season?"

"Does anyone see me?" The answer is yes! When you feel overlooked by people, you are being seen by God!

David understood what it felt like to be overlooked by people. He worked hard in the fields, taking care of the family sheep. Sadly, when it came time for the prophet, Samuel, to choose a king from David's family, his father brought all of his sons except David. Then God told Samuel, *"The Lord doesn't see things the way you see them. People judge by outward appearance, but the Lord looks at the heart. (1 Samuel 16:7b)* Samuel asked if there were any more sons, and David was named the future King of Israel. However, David did not become king right away. He had to go right back out to the fields and do the same things he was doing when nobody was watching except God. God saw both David's strengths and struggles when nobody else did. He saw everything David was going through and He sees you when you feel nobody else does! God sees your mad lunch-making skills, your struggles helping with homework, and the endless hours of hauling your kids to every game alone.

Let me encourage your heart today. You deserve a big giant crown with all the pretty jewels in the world for all that you do, and God thinks so too. *"For the Lord delights in his people; he crowns the humble with victory." Psalms 149:4*

Just Ask Lynette Gee

Longwood University Basketball

*B*eing women filled with God-given dreams, goals and expectations, we are often challenged with the daily decisions on what to turn our attention to. When the day comes that you decide to be a wife (Coach's wife at that), then later a mother; all of life's dreams as a little girl begin to align. Never in your wildest dreams could you understand the journey on which you are about to embark. Your days become filled with lots of opportunities to build and encourage your loved ones to pursue their dreams who are now on their journey.

That support comes in countless ways. Just to name a few: multiple moves, countless new school enrollments, packing and unpacking, finding churches, and getting your children acclimated to a new environment. Until one day you realize you have stopped pursuing or even yet believing in the dream and vision God has given you. How did I get here? How do you live without regret when you feel that you've lost something?

I can recall a day I was frantically searching for an item before leaving the house. I had a car full of my family filled with the expectation of where we were headed, but I ended my search not able to find my item. I entered in the car to join my family feeling lost while everyone around me was filled with joy. It didn't really matter what the item was, but I remember thinking I am helping everyone pursue their dreams but what am I doing? Feelings of guilt for even thinking this way entered in, how selfish must I be? However, as time went on I couldn't shake those thoughts.

I wonder how David must have felt knowing as a boy he had been anointed as King of Israel. I can imagine the dreams he pondered of his life ahead. However, one day he finds himself on the run from Saul. What must he be thinking; perhaps a dream lost? As I sit in the car I think this is one of many lost. They begin to mount up now, the seemingly insignificant things begin to hurt like the significant one—lost vision. How did David live during that trial? One day feeling like he was in purpose on a path to one day being King to fleeing for his life, losing the daily relationship of family and his closest friend in Jonathan. How did I get here?

My life is filled with cooking, hosting, car pooling and that dreaded homework. It's also filled with laughter and joy all around me, but sometimes all I can focus on is what seems lost. In Christ you are never lost. David's appointment was still his, and even during his journey he continued to inquire of the Lord for his direction. I almost missed it. Embracing all of what God has for me: the joys, the strength developed through the trials, the many places and new experiences, meeting wonderful people along the way, rushed car rides to school and late night runs to Walmart to buy supplies for the next day's homework project. I almost lost time spent with my loved ones, being present but not experiencing life. Trust God no matter what life brings you.

Just Ask Me

1. When are the times you feel like nobody sees you and all you do?

2. Realistically, how do you deal with those feelings?

3. How does the story of David encourage you today?

4. Write down five blessings you see around you right now?

"…and your Father, who sees everything, will reward you."
Matthew 6:18

When we run with God, we can't help but hear the plans of God…

Just Ask Isaiah

Read Isaiah's story: Isaiah 6:1-9

In our hallway, we have a big chalkboard/cork board. We call this our "Dream board." At the top are my written words "You can't be anything you want to be, but you can be anything God wants you to be." At the bottom are the dreams my kids have for their future. Right now, we have the President of the United States, a pro-baseball player, singer and the Incredible Hulk.

We would all love to know what God has in store for our family's future. What kind of season will we have? Will we still be at the same school next year? We have so many questions we want God to answer right now. I love that God is all-knowing, and because He is, He knows if He shows us what will happen tomorrow, we will miss what He wants to show us today. So what do we do in the meantime?

We should not try to figure out our future but rather get to know the One who created it. Isaiah was a prophet in the Old Testament who was simply in the presence of God and overheard a need of God. Isaiah 6:8 says, *"Then I heard the Lord asking, 'Whom should I send as a messenger to this people? Who will go for us?'" Isaiah replied to God, "Here I am. Send me."* God was not asking Isaiah to go. God was not telling Isaiah to go. Because Isaiah was searching for God through prayer, he encountered God's plans.

God wants us to do the same. He wants us to seek Him, not just as individuals, but as families. We find out what God wants when we find out who He is. We do this by reading His Word, praying to His heart, and engaging with His followers. Too often, we get so busy searching for the plans of God that we can actually miss God. We can miss lessons He is trying to teach us, plans He has for us, or love He is trying to show us. We often want from God when what we need **is** God. God does not want us to live in the past of who we used to be, or in the future of where we want to be, but in the present where He is to be.

Just Ask Stacey Hensley

Lubbock Coronado High School Baseball

*C*oaching. There's not another profession like it. Coaching's not my husband's job; it's what we do. I mean, you don't see an accountant's family walking around in "company colors" with the firm's name on the front. In 20 years, I have rarely missed a baseball game. Home, away; it doesn't matter. It's a part of who I am—who we are. And when that part is ripped away, your heart stops beating.

In June 2001, my husband was offered the head baseball job at his high school alma mater in Kansas. He had been an assistant coach in Texas for the past six years with two incredible men whose families had become part of our family. It was hard to leave, but we felt like God was leading us there. Our one-year-old would be in the same area as both sets of grandparents and would get to grow up with family just like Shawn and I had done. Shawn knew the job came with its challenges. This Kansas town had a stellar track program—double digit state championship banners hanging everywhere. Being the coach of the baseball team was not a high profile job. However, Shawn was young, energetic, and knew he could "make Liberal a baseball town." He could not imagine how anyone could not love baseball.

June 2004. We now had two boys: ages four and one. Shawn also had three tough baseball seasons behind him, but he was already making plans for how to get ready for next season. He said he needed to run up to the school, but when he walked back in the door, I knew immediately that something was wrong. He kept repeating, "I'm done." In an instant our world crashed. I'm a doer and the only thing I knew to do right then was to start packing and praying. I knew we couldn't stay because Shawn was born to coach. We had thought this place was God's plan for us for so many reasons. We felt lost. To him, his first attempt at being a head coach had resulted in the ultimate failure—being fired. All he had ever wanted to do was coach kids, but as a head coach he had to deal with so many other things that had nothing to do with teaching and coaching young people. Teaching kids the game of baseball. THAT'S what he loved. In God's perfect timing, a coaching friend called when he heard what had happened. This man had experienced a similar situation before. He told Shawn that teaching the game of baseball was what he loved and that sometimes being a head coach can get in the way of that. He told him, "There's nothing wrong with being the BEST assistant coach there is." June 2011. Our boys were 11 and 8 years old. Their shirts were being waved over their heads. I remember cheering and clapping in the 112 degree heat at Dell Diamond in Round Rock, Texas. Shawn was being presented with a silver medal as a very proud ASSISTANT coach of the District 2-5A State Runner-up Coronado Mustangs. It was all part of God's plan—ALL of it. God's perfect plan.

Just Ask Me

1. What future plans do you wish God would tell you right now?

2. As coaches wives our plans don't always match up to God's plans. Write down a time when God's plans worked out better than yours.

3. Getting to know God is the key to getting to know His plans. Write a prayer to God about your dreams, your future, and His plans.

"You can make many plans,
but the Lord's purpose will prevail."
Proverbs 19:21

Emotions are not our weakness, but what drives us to God's strength...

Just Ask David

Read about David: Psalm 5

I am an emotional being. Sometimes I try to play it off as passion, but honestly, I am emotional!

I am emotional about my husband, kids, wins, losses and while I am just putting it all out there, I am emotional about military homecomings and every walk-on football player who gets a scholarship.

As a former athlete and current coach's wife, I thought this was a weakness. However, as I grew closer to God, my creator, I learned this wasn't a weakness but a part of being created in His image. We are all emotional because we were created by an emotional God.

I had to learn that having emotions is not wrong, but letting my emotions control me can be. When our emotions control us, we can become so emotionally attached to people when we were created to be emotionally attached to God. Please understand, I am not saying we can not or should not be emotionally attached to people. I am saying that because we are so emotionally attached to people, this can often lead to unrealistic expectations from and about people. The reality is neither our husbands, friends, nor children were created to meet our spiritual, mental and emotional needs; Jesus was!

Through David and the book of Psalms, we are painted a picture of what it looks like to be emotionally attached to God:

- 1-2 Praying to God was David's first choice not his last resort
- 3 David did not expect from people what he expects from God
- 4-6 David lets God deal with his enemies so he does not have to
- 7-12 David's prayers start with his own struggles, but always end up with God's strength

Ladies, sports is an emotional profession, so when we add family and fans to the equation, we quickly realize how much we need to be emotionally attached to the one who is emotionally grounded. God is our emotional rock, so we should attach ourselves to him.

Just Ask Christina Grant

Oklahoma City Thunder Basketball

*B*eing the wife of a coach and the mother of four children can be challenging mentally, physically, as well as emotionally. I can relate to David's words in Psalms 5:1, "Give ear to my words, O Lord, consider my sighing." Over the years, there have been many sighs. My emotions have run the gambit from feelings of contentment, joy, and optimism, to feelings of fear, anger, frustration, resentment, and even loneliness. Many times, because of my husband's profession, these feelings were intensified by wins, losses, or commitments from recruited athletes.

Being married to a coach can present unique challenges when it comes to family life. I'm constantly juggling my children's activities, family activities, public life and private life, while being my husband's biggest supporter. I've learned that God allows experiences and challenges to help put us in right relations with Him or to lead us to deeper relationship with Him.

The most impactful experience occurred in 1999 when we lost our second son, who was stillborn in my eighth month of pregnancy. The emotions I felt following that experience varied day to day. In a matter of hours, the hopes and dreams we had for our unborn child were replaced with doubts, anger, fear, and often-overwhelming sadness. But looking back on it now, I can clearly see God's protective and guiding hand at work. He'd allowed my husband and I to foster relationships months earlier with faithful people who helped us get through that ordeal. To this day, I am grateful to God for allowing my husband to be home when our son was born. It took me some time to accept the fact that God didn't cause the death of our son, but He allowed it for a reason. That experience helped me to realize I had been taking God and His goodness for granted for a long time. My faith in Him had become replaced with faith in money, in wins and losses, and in commitments from recruits. Those things had taken center stage and dictated the tenor of my life.

Through that loss and other life experiences, and with the help of godly friends, I've come to understand God wants me to stay connected to Him in and through every situation. David is a great example of how I should do that. David, who feared for his life, lost his throne, and was shunned by his family and friends turned to God in the most difficult of times for direction, comfort, and strength. He cried out to God in prayer and with praise. My desire is to become emotionally connected to Him in order to have His perfect peace in my life.

Just Ask Me

1. How have you viewed your emotions in the past? As a weakness? Have you felt too much? Not enough?

2. Who or what do you tend to emotionally attach yourself to?

3. In what ways do you have expectations from people that you should be expecting from God? Fulfillment? Approval? Validation? Worth?

"No one is holy like the Lord! There is no one besides you; there is no Rock like our God."
1 Samuel 2:2

We do not have to be perfect because we are loved by perfection…

Just Ask Mary

Read Mary's Story: Luke 2:41-52

We all know those women and their families that we just can not seem to measure up to. They appear to have the perfect family pictures, and their houses are always clean. They love working out and eating kale, and of course their husband's teams are always winning championships. With each new post on Facebook or picture on Instagram, it makes us want to take our pizza-loving, back-fat bodies and crawl back to our outdated, dog-stained carpet house. We want the perfect body, with the perfect husband and kids, and the perfect life. Where do we get one of those? Let me say it loud and clear. That life does not exist!! Deep in our hearts we know this is true, but it does not keep us from trying to be the first one to achieve it.

In the story of Mary, mother of Jesus, we see the glory of being the Virgin Mary, a saint, the mother of God, but we very rarely talk about the story of her imperfections. The woman of all women, the perfect mom with the perfect son, was not all that perfect.

As we read in this story, Mary lost Jesus. She actually lost the 12-year-old son of God for three days!! The family had gone to Jerusalem for the Passover celebration and when they started to head back home, Mary and Joseph couldn't find Jesus. His frantic parents eventually found him in the temple and scolded him for not being with them. Mary is the only mother in history who can truthfully say she raised the perfect child, but that does not mean she was perfect, It meant Jesus was. She did not have to be perfect because she was loved by perfection, and so are we!

Just because you are a follower of Jesus Christ does not mean you always have to be perfect. It actually means that you can be honest and humble enough to say that you are not. You do not have to beat yourself up because you lost you son during Passover or at Walmart. Mary teaches us that being perfect does not come from doing the right things all the time, but instead by putting our faith and hope in the One who did. Jesus did not love us because we were perfect; he died for us because we were not!

Just Ask Candace Lane

Football - Archer High School, Lawrenceville, Georgia

*W*hen we first got married my husband and I were missionaries in Brazil. That is a career choice many admire, and I've even had people tell me how they wish they could do something like that. What Super Christians we must be! But I know the truth—it was one of the most stressful, humbling experiences I have ever known. I often think God used our years there to change me more than anything I could offer to our Brazilian friends. And truly, everything good does come from Him. He did use me in all my imperfection, for His glory and not mine.

Now I have the privilege of being a coach's wife, and as far as I can tell, it is very much a mission field! Not too long ago, I was up at the high school where my husband coaches, and some of our football team managers told me that when they had a family of their own one day they wanted it to be like ours. I was shocked! For some reason I was surprised that they had been observing us and even admiring our family! Then I said "be glad you don't live with us or you might change your mind!" This was **not** a good response! I should have said that what they really want is Jesus. I should have said that it's all about Him and how He changes our lives. And I should have said that if there is anything in our family you admire, it is Christ's love and grace. I missed the opportunity, but I learned a lesson:

The truth is that we are far from perfect, but in this weakness, He wants me to proclaim His powerful greatness!

I have an opportunity to have eternal impact when I understand that it is all about Him anyway so there is no need to dwell on the obvious issues I have! Those students saw something in us, and it definitely wasn't perfectly obedient kids with matching socks! I've even lost my daughter at a football game, but thankfully the policeman helped her find me!

The comparison trap is a very real thing. It chokes joy and leads to depression and it is absolutely no fun. It makes me feel like God can't use me until I reach a certain level of some kind of CrossFit, Beth Moore, Pinteresty ability. But I have experienced the freedom of honesty with other coaches' wives, something I believe that we all have to have. It is encouraging to share our similar struggles, but not with the purpose of having a pity party. Our husbands are imperfect just like us, so what if we looked to the Lord's perfection instead of dwelling on how we are not. God wants to use me—to use us! In our weakness and dependence upon Him. Nothing else. I will never have it all together, but I have Him.

Just Ask Me

1. How do you struggle with perfection in your life? Comparison? Jealousy? Being hard on yourself?

2. How does Mary's story of imperfection encourage you in yours?

3. In what ways do you need to allow Jesus to be made perfect in your weakness? Give up control? Trust issues? Relationship struggles?

"God saved you by his grace when you believed. And you can't take credit for this; it is a gift from God. Salvation is not a reward for the good things we have done, so none of us can boast about it. For we are God's masterpiece."

Ephesians 2:8-10

Sometimes the greatest blessings from God are when we are moved by God...

Just Ask Abraham

Read Abraham's Story: Genesis 12:1-9, Hebrews 11:8-10

Let's just be real...I hate to move! Well, let me clarify, I hate the process of moving. Yes, moving to a new city and new school can be exciting, but getting the house ready to sell, packing boxes, unpacking boxes and not being able to find anything because everything is in the boxes makes me stressed, tired, and grumpy.

Unfortunately, coaching families tend to move a lot. Whether you are moving because you lost a job or moving because you found a better job, change is hard!

However, while moving is never easy, it is often worth it.

Abraham lived in the land of Ur and Haran with friends and family. One day, God spoke to Abraham (he was known as Abram at the time) and said, *"Leave your native country, your relatives, and your father's family and go to the land that I will show you. I will make you into a great nation. I will bless you and make you famous, and you will be a blessing to others."* So without knowing where he was going or why, Abraham packed up himself and his wife, Sarah, and moved. We need to understand to move physically, there are times we need to be moved spiritually, too. We are not called to live by sight, but walk by faith. Because Abraham had such deep faith and trust in God spiritually, he didn't have to know exactly where he was moving physically or why.

Do we have that same depth of faith and trust?

God didn't show Abraham the end of the journey; he just told him to take the first step. We may not know where God is taking us or why; we just have to be willing to take the first step.

- Maybe the first step to change is going to church.
- Maybe the first step to change is calling a moving company.
- Maybe the first step to change is applying for your dream job.

When we are moving and growing, God is moving and working. My pastor says it this way, "Obedience is up to us; outcome is up to Him." Abraham obeyed and God came through, leading him to an amazing land in Canaan.

Wherever God is moving you, rest assured that God is moving, too!

Just Ask Caitlin Riley

University of Oklahoma Football

Being a coach's wife, I always knew the probability of a move was very likely. Being a college coach's wife, I also knew a move could be anywhere in the country. I grew up in a small west Texas town and met Lincoln, my future husband in high school. We attended Texas Tech University, 80 miles from my hometown, where he was a student coach for football. He went on to become the offensive GA for a year, before being hired as the outside receivers coach, all at Texas Tech.

This was a dream come true. We lived in a place we were familiar with, and our families were within an hour's drive. We had established everything we thought we needed in order to enjoy life: I had a job I loved teaching kindergarten, we had a church, lifelong friends and family nearby, and a familiar routine.

That all changed one January day. With a head coaching switch, all we knew would no longer be, and that inevitable move was going to happen. We had no idea when or where, but change was coming and we would be moving. Lincoln went on a couple of interviews immediately. One of our probable landing spots was exciting because it was an in-state school we knew well. Now our family would only be a quick plane ride away, but we knew people in the area and felt like the move would be seamless.

We were on a trip to check out the possible school and search for homes when Lincoln got a call. One of our beloved coaching friends and mentors was on the other end. Lincoln hung up the phone and said, "He thinks he is getting the head job at East Carolina and wants me to come as the Offensive Coordinator." My first response was, "where in the world is that?" I immediately searched the internet to find out all I could about this new, completely unfamiliar place we might be calling home soon. Sure enough Coach McNeill took the head job the next day, called, and 48 hours following the initial phone call Lincoln left our well-known home of Lubbock, Texas for the unfamiliar Greenville, North Carolina.

The Lord's hand was surely on this move. Selling our home, purchasing a new one, and moving within six weeks of taking the job was the first of many blessings we received.

While we never asked for this move, it was the best thing we could have ever done. Sure, starting over far from home is hard. There were lots of tears, but oh my there was lots of goodness to come. We moved 1300 miles from home and all we had was each other and the Lord to rely on. Our faith in the Lord and marriage grew exponentially. We found an incredible church, made dear friends, explored a completely new part of the country, had our first daughter and loved almost every minute of our five years in Greenville.

The initial heartache we experienced when leaving the familiar for the unknown resulted in the Lord moving us in ways other than the physical shift across the country.

Just Ask Me

1. Name a time when you had to move? Describe your experience during the transition? Emotions?

2. Has there ever been a time when you were moved spiritually?

3. Change is hard, but necessary in this life. What first step do you need to take toward a change God wants to make in your life today?

"Search me, O God, and know my heart; test me and know my anxious thoughts. Point out anything in me that offends you, and lead me along the path of everlasting life."
Psalms 139:23-24

We can not please everyone but we can please one…

Just Ask the Proverbs 31 Woman

Read Proverbs 31:10-31

If God created our husbands to be the "head" of our family, then he created us to be the heart. We love big. We want to be everything, to all people, all of the time. We want to help and encourage, inspire and serve. We strive to please everyone when we are called to please only one.

The Proverbs 31 woman is a woman I have read about since I was in high school. She was the woman I wanted to be as a wife, mom and ministry leader. From her servant girls to her husband and even her children, everyone in the passage seemed to love her. Eventually, though, I grew to resent her because the more I tried to be like her, the less I actually was. I was more of a Proverbs 32 woman—one her family likes most of the time. The woman that can lose her temper and feed her children hotdogs from the concession stand for the third night in a row.

The Proverbs 31 woman just seemed impossible to me, until one day I read verse 30 and my perspective changed: *"Charm is deceptive, and beauty does not last; but a woman who fears the Lord will be greatly praised."* The Proverbs 31 woman was not praised by everyone because of what she did but for whom she did it. She was not trying to please everyone, just one. God. Her love for God spilled over into every aspect of her life.

As a coach's wife, we can be pulled in so many different directions. Parents want answers from the locker room because we can be treated like a side-door into the coach's office. The booster club can want our thoughts, opinions, and help for the sports banquet. Our kids want our help with homework, activities, and friends. It can be overwhelming, but as baseball coaches say, "Keep your eye on the ball." Keep your eye on Jesus. So how do we do this? The answer is not doing more but including Jesus in everything we already do. Jesus is not the one thing at the top of our list…He is our list. When our daily focus is on Jesus, it is only a matter of time before the Proverbs 31 woman looks more and more like the woman you see in the mirror every day.

Just Ask Jamie Friesen

San Diego State University Women's Soccer

*E*arly in my career as a coach's wife, I would anxiously pace the sidelines intensely following the games. Each play, each move, each call by the ref would have me elated or depressed. This made for some interesting moments when our kids were younger and I was pulling double-duty chasing them around the stadium while hanging on every play of the game. There may or may not have been a game where our son broke his collarbone in the bleachers and I didn't immediately leave for the ER because I wanted to see the end of a close game. #proudmommoment

As a former college athlete and coach myself, I totally "get" what my husband does. I get the competition, I get the striving, the emotional undertaking of the season, the preparation, the highs and the lows. I know the girls and their stories and all they invest and put into their sport.

I also see behind the scenes to his hopes and dreams for the program and the unique way his results at his job weave themselves into the fabric of his identity as a man. And I really like winning. So I get it.

I distinctly remember when God got my attention that my stress and anxiety were not God-honoring nor healthy. It was the tail end of a close game (one that we were supposed to win, those games are the worst, am I right?) and I was doing my nervous Nancy routine behind the goal. Out of the blue, I felt God tap me on the shoulder and whisper "the result of this game is not your job. You are carrying the wrong burden."

Stunned silence. In that moment I realized that God had a job for me as a coach's wife, and my job didn't entail the outcome of the game. The final score, the final season record and the team's success were not on my plate. It was like a weight released from my shoulders.

Over the next weeks I sat with God and asked him, "ok, well what **is** my job?" And like the Proverbs 31 woman, I learned my role in the program was to love people well. Love the girls and their families. Love the facilities guys out there prepping the field for the game. Love the stat crew. Love the families of the other coaches. Love the refs. Well, let's not get carried away God. And love my husband by being his biggest fan and bringing peace and perspective into the emotional world of coaching. I am by no means perfect in this endeavor. I can still catch myself shoulders scrunched up to my ears, nervously pacing the sidelines, and I will never be that wife who isn't emotionally invested in the games and results. But I am much better about inviting God into those moments and asking Him to help me turn my eyes into living out my role as the wife of a coach and asking Him to help me live that well. Proverbs 31:25 says, "She is clothed with strength and dignity, and she laughs without fear of the future." With God's help, this will be me too!

Just Ask Me

1. Would you consider yourself a people pleaser? Why or why not?

2. Read through Proverbs 31:10-31 again. Make notes about the positive influence she had on her family, friends, servants etc.

3. Jesus said the greatest commandment was to love God first, others second, ourselves third. What are some actual steps you can take to better love each one?

"We love each other because He loved us first."

1 John 4:19

When we get too tired physically, we can fall asleep spiritually...

Just Ask Eutychus

Read Eutychus' Story: Act 20:7-12

*M*y kids and I like to go watch my husband's practice. Some of the things we hear include, "Never take a play off. Always be awake." All good advice a young man named Eutychus could have used one night while listening to Paul preach. Like Eutychus, we can be going to church, hanging out with the right people, doing all the right things, and we just get tired.

The problem with getting so tired is, we can fall asleep. We can fall asleep in our relationships, health and faith. Signs we have fallen asleep include just going through the motions and living each day without connecting with anyone including God. I know how hard and exhausting life can be but more importantly so does God. Eutychus got tired, fell out of the window and died, but that was not the end for him and it does not have to be the end for us either. Through the power of Jesus, Paul brought Eutychus back to life. That same power can wake us up when we have fallen asleep or help us find rest when we are tired.

Rest…something we hear about but have a hard time doing. Jesus says in Mark 2:27, "*The Sabbath was made to meet the needs of people, and not people to meet the requirements of the Sabbath.*" God knows we need rest; that is why he commanded us to take one. A day set aside to disconnect from the world but more importantly connect with God. When we are busy for six days and rest for one, we are showing our families, friends, and ourselves that we will do what we can and trust God to do what we can not do!

My favorite part of this story is verse 12, *"Meanwhile, the young man was taken home unhurt, and everyone was greatly relieved."* He went home "unhurt." There was no sign that showed he had gotten tired and fallen asleep: no wheelchair, no crutches, no limp. We also may have gotten tired and fallen asleep, but with Jesus we can wake up and come home "unhurt." Jesus saves us when we fall and wakes us up when we fall asleep; now rest in that!

Just Ask Amber Brown

Abilene Christine University Football

*M*oving. The coaching family's inevitable. I have always found peace with moving to a different school or even a different state. The part that has proven to be difficult for me is the process of beginning life in our new home. The positives include getting to live in different communities, among people of different cultures, try new foods and personally witness the wonders of God through His beautiful creation. However, moving is also hard. When moving day arrives you are once again a stranger in a new town. Finding your place in your new community can be challenging. Of course from the outside it seems that we are set up with our own community in the other wives and coaches and that is true. However, we not only want to be a part of the coaching family, we want to establish friendships within our community. We want to be as much of a light to those in our area as we can, while we have the time with them.

Here is where I put so much pressure on myself. I must quickly find a lifelong friend, a new church home, great group of friends for my children, bible study group and sports teams for my children. When I say "quickly find these things," I am actually meaning the first week of being in our new home. That is not asking much, right? This is why I so desperately need to rest in Christ. I am a mess. When I should be heavily relying on God in these times I often continue in auto drive. I would go through the motions daily, afraid of the unknown and too stubborn to take a moment to come to my knees and ask my gracious Savior to help me rest. I wanted to be the best I could be for everyone and ensure the transition was perfect. Unfortunately, it took me a couple of moves to realize what was happening. I would take over by trying to control every aspect of the new location and take God's plan into my own hands. I wanted Him to be proud of how I was following His plan, and I wanted it to work perfectly to my design. It became about me while I was trying to make it about Him. I was tired.

This could not continue. Before one of our recent moves, as I was praying about our new locations, I knew I did not want to handle it on my own. I didn't want to leave the next place feeling exhausted and having had no growth. I asked God to show me why the beginning was so hard for me and to help me rely on him during those times. He confirmed over and over to me to let things flow, to trust in Him and to let Him work His plan from the beginning to the end. So I prayed. A lot. I prayed that God would give me contentment in His plan and that He would help me to press forward even when I felt like I was not doing enough. I continually asked God to give me the strength to let others help, to humble me to see that I cannot do it alone. I realized God is ready to use me as I am. I can let go of the control. I can say no when things get overwhelming. I can give Him my burdens, my control, my need to please others. I can rest in Him.

Just Ask Me

1. Describe what life is like when you get tired physically, emotionally, mentally, and/or spiritually.

2. When you get tired how do you "fall asleep" in your relationships with your husband? Kids? Jesus?

3. What is one thing you can start today to "wake up"? (Quiet time with Jesus, plan a date night with your husband, make a memory with your child etc.)

"I know all the things you do, and that you have a reputation of being alive-but you are dead. Wake up! Strengthen what little remains…."
Revelation 3:1-2

If your opponent can get you to doubt your identity,

he can get you to doubt your purpose...

Just Ask Jesus

Read Jesus' Story: Matthew 3:13-17, 4:1-11

As coach's wives, we often find ourselves in an identity crisis. Let me encourage you; it is possible to be part of a great team and still maintain our identities as individuals. Unfortunately, we face an opponent who would love for us to doubt our identity or to forget it completely.

Jesus faced this same battle with the same opponent. Right before Jesus met his enemy, God declared him, "my dearly loved Son, who brings me great joy." The very next thing his opponent, Satan, did was try to make Jesus doubt himself by saying, "if you are the son of God...." Once we are followers of Jesus, his enemy becomes our enemy. Satan whispers the same trash-talking garbage in our ears in attempt to doubt our identities in Christ. It may sound like, "if you are child of God,"or "if you are not a failure, all phrases that contradict everything God has told us we are through his son, Jesus. Romans 8:15-16 says, *"So you have not received a spirit that makes you fearful slaves. Instead, you received God's Spirit when he adopted you has his own children. Now we call him, "Abba, Father." For his Spirit joins with our spirit to affirm that we are God's children."*

We are daughters of the King, a part of God's Team! If our opponent can get us to doubt our identity, then he can get us to doubt our purpose. Our purpose is to do great things for God with the individual gifts and talents given to us by God, and that includes you! It is so easy to forget our gifting when so much focus can be on our husbands. You and your husband are a team working together toward the same goal using your individual gifts. If your gift is to bake, then bake. If your gift is to teach, then teach. Maybe you organize, so organize. As a child of God, you were created for greatness because you were created by greatness.

Karen Wheaton said it this way, "Satan's greatest fear is that you would believe what God says about you." God can use anybody at anytime to do anything! Why not your husband, and why not you? I believe God's greatest joys are to watch his children, sons and daughters, using their gifts to further His Kingdom.

Just Ask Kelly Loepp

SMU Football

*M*y name is Kelly Loepp, and I have been a coach's wife since 2008. We have two wonderful little boys, Easton and Brooks. When I met my husband, Jess, I knew he was made for me. He was without a doubt everything I had prayed for and I knew he would be a wonderful husband and spiritual leader. Life as a coach's wife was pretty easy in the beginning, I was an elementary school teacher who spent about as much time in my classroom as Jess spent in the football office. Once we had our boys, though, so much changed and the job of being a coach's wife became a lot harder than I could have ever imagined. I had always had wonderful friends I worked with but shortly after I decided to be a stay at home mom I felt those relationships fade. I started to really struggle being lonely and feeling like I was losing my identity. During the week I am mommy, and on the weekend I am Mrs. Loepp or Coach Loepp's wife, but I wasn't Kelly anymore; at least that was how I started to feel.

I started hearing that voice inside my head say, "you aren't important anymore," and by that voice I mean Satan. Satan was doing a great job of making me feel pretty worthless and alone. Moving brought the opportunity of making new friends and turning this feeling of loneliness around. I decided to get a teaching job again and told myself how fantastic this was going to be, never praying about it or really seeking what God had for me. As the new school year started and Jess' football season began I found myself in total overload. I was leaving for school at 6:30 so that I could drop the boys off at childcare and get to work before the bell rang. I spent all day there and usually picked up the boys around 5:30. We were all miserable, and I finally had to come to terms with the fact that I could not be the mom I wanted to be while being the teacher I wanted to be. I resigned from my job and once again stayed home with the boys. I felt wonderful about it at first but Satan slowly started creeping back in and reminding me I wasn't that important. Slowly I started realizing not only had I lost my identity but also my purpose.

I am God's creation. The Lord created me for a purpose and I don't have to look far to find my identity, I just need to look to Him for it. I meet so many wonderful people with Jess' job: players, coaches, wives, parents… so if I wasn't important why would he put so many people in my path? Sometimes life doesn't have to be as difficult as we make it. Exodus 9:16 says, "*But I have raised you up for this very purpose that i might show you my power and that my name might be proclaimed in all the earth.*"

Just Ask Me

1. What lies from your opponent have you been believing about yourself?

2. Where do you typically find your identity? Mom? Wife? Teacher?

3. So often our purpose is tied to our identity. Knowing you are a child of God, how does that change your purpose?

4. Write a prayer asking God to help you defeat your opponent.

"And since we are his children, we are his heirs. In fact, together with Christ we are heirs of God's glory."
Romans 8:17